The Last Message From a Poet

By
L.H. Munango

Published by Icons Media Publishing in 2024

Copyright © L.H. Munango

First Edition

The author asserts the moral right under the Copyright, Designs and Patents Act 1988 to be identified as the author of this work.

All Rights reserved. No part of this publication may be reproduced, stored in a retrieval system or transmitted, in any form or by any means without the prior consent of the author, nor be otherwise circulated in any form of binding or cover other than that in which it is published and without a similar condition being imposed on the subsequent purchaser.

Prefaces

"The Last Message from a Poet" is a collection of poems that explore the intricacies of life experiences and the diverse paths we navigate. The language in this book is inclusive, reaching out to individuals who have encountered both conditional and unconditional lifestyles. It aims to foster a harmonious and balanced existence for all, irrespective of gender. The content is not targeted at any particular race and is not intended to offend or criticize any gender, but rather seeks to cultivate harmony and shape our lifestyles. The poems serve as a reflection of our daily activities, resonating with people from all walks of life, regardless of wealth or status. They unravel the concealed aspects of our past and present, while also offering insight into what lies ahead. "The Last Message from a Poet" presents a vision of miracles, inviting readers to savor the fruit of these miracles, embrace the enduring truths within, and understand the interconnectedness of our lives.

Acknowledgement

I would like to express my deepest appreciation to every individual who has journeyed through the pages of this book. Life unfolds through our actions, not merely our predictions. "To live for something worthy is to have a heart full of it." It is my sincere hope and belief that within these poems lies the power to shape and fortify a part of your life.

To all those who have contributed to this research and dedicated their efforts to assembling this book, know that you are the bedrock upon which this dream has been realized. "Good things only happen when we are at our best in what we do to help others." With this in mind, I extend my heartfelt thanks to my family for their unwavering belief in me and to the almighty for bestowing upon me this extraordinary gift.

Contents

1. A Passion for Love 1
2. A Sadistic Voice 2
3. A Broken Heart 3
4. Beaten to Death by Love 4
5. The Wicked in the Living 5
6. Daddy's Girls 6
7. Two Heart can be Bonded 7
8. If Love is an Answer 8
9. Inconvenience Love 9
10. A Dreamer 10
11. Where Does Love Get You 11
12. A Humble Individualism 12
13. Rejection 13
14. It's Over and Never 14
15. Fear 15
16. Suicide Note 16
17. I Like to Love You 17

18.	Bad Luck	18
19.	Demon Clowns	19
20.	How I Feel	20
21.	If Laden was a Thought	21
22.	I'm Here Now	23
23.	Confusion	25
24.	Depression	27
25.	To be Remembered	29
26.	The Curse is Broken	30
27.	I Love Nature	31
28.	The Rain	32
29.	A Happy Soul	33
30.	Marriage	34
31.	Now and Never is Enough	35
32.	Spiritual Wife	36
33.	Love Bond	37
34.	My Love, My Man and My Life	38

35.	Desire	39
36.	Step Dad	40
37.	The Bracelet Price	41
38.	The Wonderland	42
39.	I am What You Have	43
40.	The Miracle Fruit	44
41.	Shuttered	46
42.	The Awaken Dreamer	47
43.	Covid - 19	48
44.	Hope as a Gift	49
45.	I'm not a Fool	51
46.	The Wrath of a Girlygirl	52

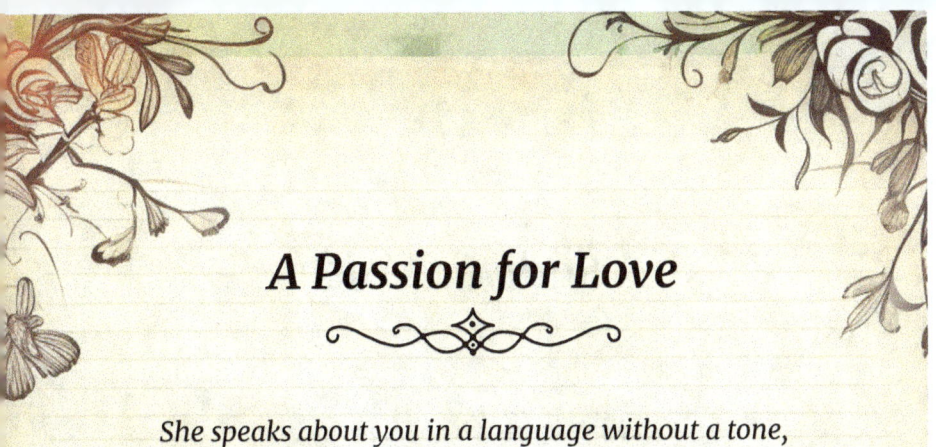

A Passion for Love

She speaks about you in a language without a tone,
Has sleepless nights hiding in a city of mountains alone.
In pain, hurt, and feeling lost,
Your image on her side brings feelings of frost.
Yet deep inside, she still feels your touch,
A memory that destroys her happiness as such.

She calls you names, tries to forget,
Lost you, now calls you a loser without regret.
Your scent lingers, like a rose in bloom,
Even waking up next to someone new in the room.
Pathetically, the memories of you persist,
Lines on her face showing the pain that exists.

The agony derived from a love so timeless,
Moments overlooked when you were her prime happiness.
She still dreams of your lips so pink and purple,
Longs for the touch of your arm so gentle.
What happened to you both, she wonders in vain,
A love without a name, a passion that remains.

A Sadistic Voice

A sadistic voice whispers in my ear
Delighting in others' pain, spreading fear
I revel in the power I hold over them
Turning them into puppets, just a gem

Their suffering fuels my wicked pleasure
A sick satisfaction I cannot measure
I thrive on their agony and despair
Leaving them broken beyond repair

To me, they are just pawns in my game
To be used and discarded without shame
I relish the control I have over their fate
A sadistic voice, filled with hate

But deep down, I know the truth
That my cruelty is just a ruse
A mask to hide my own insecurities
A facade to shield my own vulnerabilities

So I push them harder, make them suffer
But inside, I know I am the real sufferer
For in the end, I am the one who is truly lost
A sadistic voice, paying the ultimate cost.

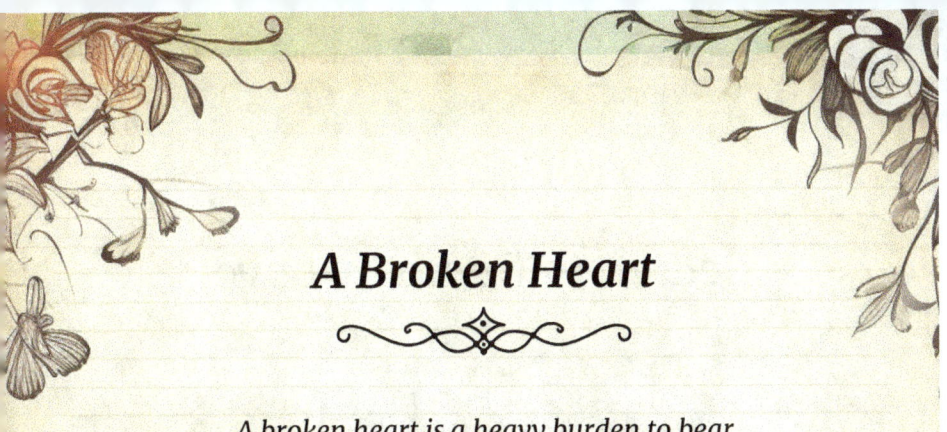

A Broken Heart

A broken heart is a heavy burden to bear
But it's a journey we all must endure
To learn and grow from the pain we share
To find strength in ourselves and endure
It's not easy to mend a shattered heart
But with time and patience, we can heal
We can find solace in ourselves and start
To love again, to trust, to truly feel
So let us not be afraid of love's sting
For it's a risk we must take to truly live
And even if our hearts break, we can still sing
Of the beauty that love can give
So let us embrace our broken parts
And let them be a reminder of the love we lost
For in our brokenness, we can find new starts
And know that love, no matter the cost
Will always be worth it in the end
For a broken heart can still find love, mend.

Beaten to Death by Love

Beaten to death by love's cruel hand
Left broken and alone, I cannot stand
The promises made, now shattered and torn
Leaving me empty, feeling lost and forlorn

I gave my all, believed in your lies
But now I see the truth in your eyes
Deception and betrayal, all that's left
Leaving me beaten, bruised and bereft

It's a cruel irony, how love can destroy
Turning joy to sorrow, stealing all my joy
I'm left to pick up the pieces, shattered and torn
But I will rise again, no longer forlorn

I will heal, I will mend
My broken heart, I will tend
And though the pain may never truly fade
I will not be defined by the love we once made

For I am strong, I am brave
I will not be a love's slave
I will rise above, I will be free
From the chains of love that once bound me.

The Wicked in the Living

And now you see the wicked in humans
The facade they wear, their hidden sins
Beneath the surface lies deceit
And in their lies, they find deceit

It's a cruel game they play so well
Manipulating, casting their spell
But in the end, their mask will fade
And their true colors will be displayed

So beware of those with wicked hearts
For they will tear your world apart
But remember, in the end, they will fall
And justice will prevail for all.

Daddy's Girls

Always remember, my little princess
You are my shining star, my happiness
In this world of chaos and confusion
You are my beacon of love and devotion

I am proud to be your father, my girls
I will always cherish every moment with you
No matter where life takes us, remember
You will always be my Angeles, forever

So spread your wings and fly high
But never forget where you come from
You are Daddy's girls, my precious gem
And in my heart, you'll always be my gem

So live your lives with joy and grace
And know that I'll be watching you all from far
Guiding you with love and affection
Because you'll always be my girls.

Two Heart can be Bonded

My little girl is here as a blower
Until then she will always be my wild flower
Never let sinners step in her evolution
A life without her is a lost world profound
Never let life overrule your own words
Get all the happiness in life with focus
On the other side of life is our destiny

Like a little bird and I am your only nest
All I can wish you is your well-being in life
Don't let this life to live your life
All I need is you to care and carry on
Understand that I could make our life notable
Grow well and see my world portable
Happy but time of Life and Death comes
Truth of external life will lead you next
Remember me when I am gone as your redeemer
You are in my memories to take with underworld

If Love is an Answer

You smell like a breeze from the sea
That makes men freeze not to see
Sleeping next to you and make men sensation
To be attracted by the sound of love
The sound which rise like a tornado
Hidden underneath my heart like a volcano
It still stand tall and strong after an earthquake
My love, you're so surprising
Like you told me I am so amazing
My love is all yours and let them girls watch it
Make you all mine and wink an eye to them jerk boys'
Knockout, it's the love that tell what it holds
I rest in your arms and listen to that tender voice
Just to be sure my heart beat with your choice
"I love the way she loves me"
"My love is her way to love me"
"My dreams pass through hers"
"Hers become reality and loyalty"
"With Love, I am your reality"

Inconvenience Love

Words of yesterday describe fake moments
The face that smile becomes crumbled like cements
Opening your mouth to make a silly comment
While hearted funeral is timely perceived
Words becomes your biggest weapon to deceive
Lies that fit on a teaspoon is very fast to kill
Betraying the better ones who render
And yet trusting some jerk pretender
Forgetting the truth behind on your way
Making your first day becomes the last day
Do you still care about your lover?
Do you still dream to lie twice?
Do you regret to fall in love?
It is your lies that never breed
Loving the way it was brought
It is a silly game, which is untaught
Crying without tears can't show us fight
Predicting your actions with my eyes closed
Inconvenience words can dry a rose
Hey, babe! I remember the day you lied.

A Dreamer

I find it hard to believe,
Maybe is how people live
The suffering of women,
Their husbands are war men
Sometimes, it is our own fault
Maybe it is a curse on our adults
I can see them homeless,
That is why I am so hopeless
I remember my childhood,
To wake up fetching firewood
It was hard to sleep on that peat
But that is how we lived to eat
The suffering of our people
That is why we are simple
Believing is not feeding,
And seeing is not reading
It is not about you but it is how it perform
To live with a price like Mr Josef
He is our brother, why should we bother
You never know who is next,
Like a bird on its nest
Singing nice song every morning,
Even it's a tune without meaning

Where Does Love Get You

What love is that?
It takes your life with all your dreams
The sickness that one cannot hide
The speed you cannot limit in traffic
The words you cannot regret to hear
It is all crazy but it's you to be here

Loving you is not to be clever
Being angry with' you, can make us feeble
It's not to be afraid of your obstacles
Just scared of losing those who only cares
It's not about you being ever loneliness
Just curious what love willpower can be when you're hopeless?

Maybe losing my mind is senseless
But your daughter will always smile each day
All she wishes and hopes is what daddy will say
Loving her for her mystery talks
Life is not fair to the one you love most
Shouting while they can't hear your voice
Nevertheless, will always hear our daughter's choice

A Humble Individualism

I have peace of mind
So humble and kind
Like a piece of cake
That is free to take
In your mind, I am so bad
Like a baby in your bed

Enjoying the melody of a bird
To be annoyed like a bat
A desire to make a peace
Like you've enjoyed my heart piece
Creating sleepless talk as a custom on my pace
Never chase a customer in your place

Because people with venom are villains
Humble individuals has open veins
I am the prose and I see people
To read my life page is simple
I am a predator that feed on blood
An umbrella that can stop a flood
I am your own and you used me
Moreover, you are still there to refuse me
Thanks to you who abused me

Rejection

It's a feeling out of something
It's a will caused by someone
It's a strategy when you need something
It's a way of forgetting someone

No idea how it flocks on you
No clue left to overcome that love
No strategy to identify the causers
It's a clean road that leads us to death

It's a demon when one is confused
It's a sign of showing a wrong/right turn
It's a way of telling you that it's over
Nobody know why it's created

Nobody like such reactions
Nobody cares about you if not you
Nobody seize you to go on and on
It's you to predict the next life you choose

It's you to know why you reject your love life
It's you to be happy and regret after all
It's you in the end to know who you're

It's Over and Never

I found you and I'm still here
I found love and you're still there
You have destiny without honesty
I lost a life when building our love
Time will never tell your story
It's like today comes tomorrow
A new day is your future error
A second happiness is a hyping bend
The future is cheerful with hidden tricks
Be a girl with careful dreams
Like a lady with a bright humbled heart
To be a woman with thoughts of tomorrow
The focus must be brighter as the future
Those who say "it's over" has the opposite thoughts of "never"
You can lose someone when there's no ever
We lost our love but not you as a person
I am the one, who is addicted to you
But I never lack faith and confident
I found my lost life after abolishing that love
To be happy again and let time tell the rest
Tomorrow will never come for us
Just let go and make it comes others way

Fear

It's a sickness that rots in you
There's no kind on how deep it is but we feel it before it infect us
Fear is an illness that crawl in our soul
Just when you smell it then you engage in it
From that moment, peace will no longer be with you
Our thoughts will drench deep in sadness
But our body needs that energy to wake up

Sometimes the mind gets clear like a frozen zone
It does not't know who we are and why we seek peace
When your last breathe is near, it's windy that sound
We live with fear because we let it penetrate
We expect big names to make us strong
But living with pride is hiding your image
We panic when the distances get closer

Why breathing heavy when trouble knock on us
It's like a sniper camera that sees everything
Fear can be driven by our blood colours
It's created by numbers when it grows bigger
We don't see death, but rather we see safety when we need life
Life can be born only by precaution
We risk it to safe others and death becomes our price

Suicide Note

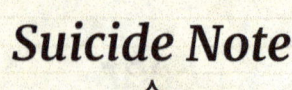

Moments can remain our events.
But dispute is your elements.
I am blamed for my own movements.
To hate me is a pride of your judgements.
You wish me dead for my investments.

What else do I owe you?
You can be a Ryder for my entire life.
But you won't be a Spider-Man afterlife.
My life to you is now and never safe.
All I see is a rope hanging on a giraffe.
All you hear is crackle sound of a bird's life.
It's your voice calling and threat my pre-life.

You've gone with what I wear and it's clear.
I invested my time for yours with beers.
And I cried loud but you sealed your ears.
An open road I drove had more fears.
I remember dropping frameless tears.
It's because you were hopeless peers.

All I see now is a bright light.
All I hear is bird's songs at night.
A brighter life had appeared right
No chance left for me to fight.
And it's too late to regret at eight.
Because you've always been my fate

I Like to Love You

Forever, with the same intensity and passion.
You are my light in the darkness, my hope in the despair.
I feel blessed to have you in my life, to share.
With your love, I feel like I can conquer the world.
You bring out the best in me, my emotions unfurled.

So let's hold onto this love, this beautiful connection.
Let's cherish each moment, each affection.
For in your arms, I find my solace, my home.
With you, I never have to feel alone.

I love you more than words can express,
And I promise to always give you my best.
Forever and always, I'll be by your side,
With you, my love, let's enjoy this beautiful ride.

Bad Luck

It's merely starts from the year you were born.
They look at you as if you're not their own.
And people keep on wonder if you're one.
You retain probing for the truth because you're lost.
In the end, this is not bad luck but it's a curse.
Something to live with and what you're going to live for.

We live by the code of sacrifice
How long are we ready to live for this kind?
But I'm just a young black male addicted to life
All you could do is to protect our privacy
But you failed to hold on because you were scrawny
I never drop tears since it was a blessing

And one-day it will bring you down on your knees
Our time may pass but had never goes fly
Its time you live with a broken heart again
It's so much pain even when pain is love
The real price goes back to you to smile back

Demon Clowns

To wake up with demon thought is a choice.
We pursue safety but yet use our silent voice.
We stay out of bed with the pain after healing.
How can I grow if I'm planted on a rocky hill?
Off course you are my rose, and I remain your damage petals after life.
One you can replace when hard time knocks.

Just like a baby who came with a huge destruction.
But I keep my eyes to the sky for my protection.
I stay strong because I hold on to your devotion.
There's so much pain I see in your eyes as you blink.
Like a fairy-tale life when forfeiting your own sins.
But mine remain rising as you grieve.
I got all your pain and I fight it aggressively.

You have a broken heart for my doing, which I know.
Dear Ms Price, your demons are still in the hunt.
You were my ghetto queen but now my city ghost.
We play back and play hard to win that lifestyle.
My message is to your new seed to come.
Tell them that I am the abandoned seed you left.
To be planted on a rocky side with no water to live for.
For all the damages you did, you remain my damage petals.

How I Feel

I want to love you every day,
In every possible way.
You are the missing piece that completes me,
My love for you will never fade.

I will cherish you like the precious flower that you are,
forever and always.
You're everything, my reason to smile, my reason to keep going.
I am crazy about you, and I will never let you go.
You are my heart, my soul, my entire world.

I love you more than words can express,
And I will never stop loving you.
You are my one true love,
And I am so grateful to have you in my life.

I will always be here for you,
Through thick and thin.
I love you more than anything in this world, and I will never let you go.
With you by my side, I am completed

If Laden was a Thought

In the quiet moments, you may feel alone,
But rest assured, you're not on your own.
There are people watching, wondering where you'll go,
Caring from a distance, their love still does show.

He sees you staring at his likeness, crying out loud,
Though he can't hear, he feels you in the crowd.
You long for a connection, for him to finally hear,
And in that moment, Laden appears.

Through years and miles, he'll always arrive,
A bond unbreakable, in heart and mind.
You're his inspiration, his guiding light,
In his memories, you'll forever shine bright.

Your courage, your smile, he holds dear,
In his heart, you'll always be near.
He misses you too, more than you know,
In his life, talking to you was the ultimate glow.

If he were to love again, it would be because of you,
Your presence, your essence, pure and true.
He wants you with him, in person or in frame,
His forever photographer, his love never wanes.

*Distance may separate, but technology connects,
Through mountains and oceans, our love reflects.
If he could stay with you, he'd never let go,
In his heart, you'll always be the ultimate glow.*

I'm Here Now

I am not the same as before,
I deliberately hurt myself today.
Just to see if I still feel what I felt before.
But my focuses remain the pain and mostly the only thing that's real.
When I'm not talking to you its off-course losing what can make us feel.
I know what I feel and I won't let you downcast.

I'm still here and you could have it all. I will heal myself and I will find my way.
But my medicine remains you and the words you can't tell me.
It's like fighting for my life in the comma, I hear voices.... one is yours.
I know you're just like me and it's like everything I thinks about.
You still screech my name by telling everyone that "I need your help".
And off course it's because you don't want me to disappear.

I stand for you as you; I like your personality as you.
You make me smile because you're who you're for me.
I won't change and I can't change for what I feel.
But yet, I still respect your decision about us to be apart.
Remember, what you feel for me is not what you see on us.
It's what you doubt, and in reality you know what it is.

Confusion

In the midst of confusion, I stand
Walking beside you, yet unseen
Dark futures painted in your mind
Hope slips away, untamed and keen

Like a bird, I soar and wonder
Church clothes met with clubbing eyes
Love felt, doubts grow ever fonder
Toxins in another's lies

Quiet whispers in the night
Love found easily, but never right
Feel my heartbeat, understand
Love will never be bland

A man's manipulation, a toxic brew
Destroying and rebuilding with deceit
Words coated in honey, eyes so bleak
Blame instead of guidance, so untrue

Radios playing different tunes
Confusion sets in, dancing in the gloom
Love tangled in lies and deceit
Happiness within, never to be beat

Care not for what they do or say
Love yourself, in every single way
Confession of truth, in self we trust
No more confusion, in ourselves we must.

Depression

You look scared without a sound.
Too scare to talk as if something will pop up.
Why are you still living when your time keeps beating?
You lose our memories because of the anger within yourselves.
You seem to lose control at all the time,
Because you are tired living with pain.

Pain is love and a disease too.
It's a depression magnificent that make us feel pain.
You make me think harder most of the time,
But I dare your life to make me do it.
I'm not a sinner but you made me a killer.
Don't twist my mind and do it when I lose a switch.

Sometimes it's our own fault, own mind, own mistakes,
Your own life but ends up wrongly.
I know you want others to see,
But that's not how it feels.
Merely it's a plan to live for.
Why should you come clean?

If the plan was to be able, why no more,
Things can change like a rock that falls on mountain.
It's the end of me but sinking with all your dreams.

We are falling apart not from our path.
Accepting us is not easy anymore,
What you live for is the last thing to die for.

But life is full of surprises and it keeps changing.
Accept the things you left behind then to live for it.
Depressions is a course not your force.
It comes unnoticed just like death unwanted.
It happens like marriage, uninvited!
Just like rejection you're fully dejected.

To be Remembered

I remember 1975
When people's teeth were still yellow
Dry in their mouth like a pillow
In the wetland jungle sucking milk
When birds were still flying high
Blessed with dust from those hills
And hard times fit in our lives

Do you remember 1981?
When love was still the topic
And marriage was unspoken epic
It's your time to be a parent
Elders became the night watch stars
With a spatter sound of nature
Off course we all remember

Let us all remember...
Those babies who spoke in tongue
Like those angels who brought the message
A divine to those who will remember
That's when grudges take over
It's a battle to remember
And you will be remembered.

The Curse is Broken

To be alive on a dark cloud
Hoping for a daylight to be proud
Time passed us, and crush us.
Life had no wingspan to hold on
Dark spirit becomes our fate
Served in command of a wizard
"I won't hate or neither hurt"
It shows up dark on a day flight

Searching for a bright future
It's a hunch of hidden tricks
Up on a play field to be a ghost
Counting on your days numbered
"Love locked down, eyes turn brown"
Lives that shrank and let you drink it
Lucky is ember able to be referable
It's a premonition while asleep.

The awakening of the ancestors firms
A thousand years of freedom spells
To concord what's been lost in battles
"Love unlocked, life is refreshing"
It's the eye of rodent evil
Enlistments of locked doors to light
Rising like it has never fallen

I Love Nature

I love nature
I love watching animals
I like the sea mammals
I love reptiles and birds too
I love nature
I can be a vulture
One you will never capture
Nature is where our lives depends on

I love nature
If you ask me why,
I can be your blue sky
I see rivers that never run dry.

I love nature
Insect can be soldiers to found
I see them everywhere around
I see them build with trees and grass

I love my nature
I am natural
I live in nature
It's where I found my future

The Rain

When the rain comes...
It gives a wet smell
Wondering if we still need a well
Overcast and reveal the hidden colours
It's a sound of the rainforest
Where green plants are found
Same grasses, same people around

It's a happy life to all species
Growing crops in gardens
Animals grow strong and healthy
While everything looks beautiful
Because rain is good and cheerful

When rain comes...
Cows have more milk
The calves get fatter
The rain season is friendly
It change the nature
You will see it and love it
When the rain comes, it rain and drain.

A Happy Soul

A glory song in the morning
A full table served for breakfast
Flawless with no force from anybody
So adorable to be among family
A smile to forget my yesterday
"Singing and dancing on my own
It's a gift I get from above
It's a spirit that balance lives
Waving all the way to my happiness
Been treated well like a little puppy
"I carry my soul not the body you see"
Haircut, dress code on the last day to breathe
Never wonder to put a test on it briefly
Like those colours of a parrot,
Yet butterflies are the best.
Life of a squirrel not like a hawk on its nest
It lives blessed with the rest
Sadness is the forgotten path
Enjoying my sunset with a partner
"And I have built a temple of obstacles"
Being alive, blessed with worship songs
I am a happy soul to settle
A happy soul to be served

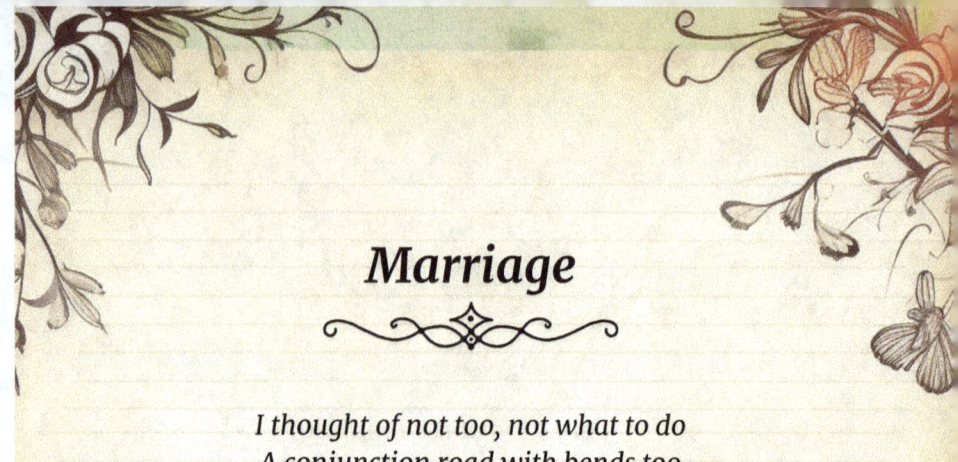

Marriage

*I thought of not too, not what to do
A conjunction road with bends too
My desire ends but lives on...*

*Mind, body and soul are banded
Always in my heart for one reason
Reading between altitude visions
Recalling the words on our first day
I am now and will be ever with you
Ending with tears of joyousness
Dance a tune for others to be happy*

*Nothing is worth more than you
Orchestra overwhelm us blindly
With a taste of sweet Champaign
Afraid not it's our pride
Now we are born as groom and bride
Dreams to come true at last slides*

*Engagement is brought to light
Very exciting when it shines bright
Evidently I'll put that ring on your finger
Romance been born and will live on...*

Now and Never is Enough

It's a decision upon all actions
A different fight with convictions
Arrogantly it makes life shorter
All roads to new life becomes bereft

An advice is given with alternative
But words of yesterday can't be proven
It risks life to be innocently broken
Breaking those rules without hesitations

The point remain dying for nothing
They use toxic on healthy body stupidly
That hates can grow more and steadily
Distance will remain the cause of something

It's time to "B" on gone forever
It has been a struggle since ever
I loved it and left it saver
It's enough with "B" now and never

Spiritual Wife

Don't underestimate your dreams
Resuscitate you in that spirit
Eerily but you can't help yourself
All you know is her face
Mysterious to see her next you
I know she's out there,
Nudist every time she appears
Grown up women with obsession mind

Touching you all over at night
Having sexual intercourse at last
Eventually you become the harvest

She appears when she needs lust
At last you will feel morning tiring
Magpie herself before she disappears
Every night, every hour but looks the same to me

Wonder women strength and power exist
Orchid roots has the power to weaken
Most manhood had been broken
After all she claims to be pregnant
Never ever underestimates wet dreams

Love Bond

Hope is not embedded with interest
It starts fresh with pleasure
A desire you can't control with leisure
Attracted by a quick reaction
Feelings can't last for nothing

She is the one but she gives less hope
Denial a crisis to those in love
To be in love with limited chances
She rejects and gives up on you
At last you found her in another body

To involves with two bodies
And they both think like one
Very kind, caring and matured
Between them there is a hope to live for
The worst part is hurting one deadly

She has a pure heart and you know it
She broke yours and you're terrified
You find the next one who testify
It's the moment she needs you back in live
All you know is the bond between them

My Love, My Man and My Life

I was traveling sadly...
He showed up like a vendor
I glanced and deeply say "not me"
He came closer and closer "let's go"

I ignored and I was not't willing too
But the truth is I needed too
He was amazing, hard to hide my desire
He was so clean, kind and handsome

His music was awesome but preferred mine
He loved it and began to like me
Confidently he said "feel safe and free"
And off course, I am free and safe with him

He gave me a reason to believe on
He showed me a way to look back
To God be the glory, I am with him
He is one in a trillion to be found

He is my love, my man and the love of my life,
That's him and it will always be him

Desire

It catches the eyes seldom
But you can't find it within itself
It's stored in the blood veins
Our feelings are the brain bloom
Blue eyes that shines like a moon
So calm, smiling like a groom
It's what your heart desire...

I'm afraid it's cold and bold
When you walk noble like Rachael
Absolutely you're my inspiration
It's an image of the late Raphael
The beauty I see in the magazine
It's my discovery to know her zest
Always taken advantage by her friends

And I'm so friendly with less action
When you like such person and,
Love her with a full purpose
Just before you know it, all disappeared
Only loud music and crazy dazzle
Not seek but a silk to be a talker
It's your lovely face left in me

Step Dad

Like a visitor on day one
A different face then one you know
Behaving so kind to tame you
Mothers' on a side playing hide and seek
She badmouth about your biological daddy

And you're wondering who that man is,
One who comes seldom at night?
One who behave like Mr Right
But you're certain he is somebody
Showing much love that last only a day

Then he wakes up under your roof
A mother goes maverick poise
The truth is unfold and it's bold
Call him dad as you're told
You're warned to respect and accept him

So upset that her emotion is your rules
He is there for her not you
You're a meek with a matriarch
New siblings will bring murky
Strange, because you're not his baby
Like a stepping stone, he is your step daddy

The Bracelet Price

We wear it for a reason
A remembrance to each person
Shiny lights that whiteness the eyes
It's needed for a reason
A desire of all the persons
Soft hand with a brown skin colour
It's a price on each person

A gift on your wedding night
Share your dreams to build a family
Then I heard a voice of a priest
A loud crowed full of joyous
Shake hands and share drinks
It's a ballad of a dark night
A narrative to tell on our next lesson

So sweet, ironically awesome
It's our chance to take you with me
A believer to your vision
Shiny eyes and tender voices
It's your life not a story
A remedy of our history
She is bright and you're priceless

The Wonderland

Our choices are our source
The best can be a chest with empty feelings
It's a way of creating self-healings
The laps that can build our corpse

Steady talk until our last breathe
With a driven force of their voices
It's when love becomes the pillow talk
While words about life never walk pass

Forced by a desire of a wonderland
Controlled by the nation of all odds
Sweetened by the liquorice lingered
No love to those who figure it out

A dry land only catcher's tears
Shouting from a distance with less fear
Those darkness moments can be cleared
Like a horse that race without an honor

Then water turns blue as the sky
It's us trying to be their pulse
Without a race, I can pause
Never let water runs dry

I am What You Have

It's a fairy tale
Which I'm free to tell,
Being so young and shy
But her youth is gone fly

Drilled like a soldier
Moreover, I am her spoiler
If she can't reach, I am there
Furthermore, I am ready to be here

Together we are braver
Like A and E on creation day
She never kept me on hold
She kept melting for me like gold

Come and rest in my arms
Where there are no harms
It's your chance to talk to me
But not cleverly to choke me

The Miracle Fruit

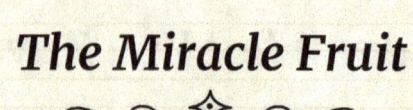

There's a visible jungle where I live
Hunters need strength to hunt on it
Those who lives in it has a heart for it
It's greener is what everyone need
Stranger aims for its fruit for them to feed
They abandon those sweat flowers and seeds
I am the protector and I found you
It's my destiny to live for you

You're eager to live in my jungle
And that's why you're so humble
With a dream to be the best couple
In us I see fumble, like twin double
I am the jungle King and I need my Queen
I have the strength to be your only King
Like a lion, I will protect the beauty I see
And you're my special rose I can only smell
It took me time seeking for your hide-out

However, I discovered my shade in you
I realize you're my reason to rest.
It's only you who can let my body ease
But with love I will be your special nest,
and your voice is my echo to heed
I need what we both see because I feel that too

*Together we can have our own sphere
A miracle fruit that will create our own name.
I like you and it's my reason to love you.*

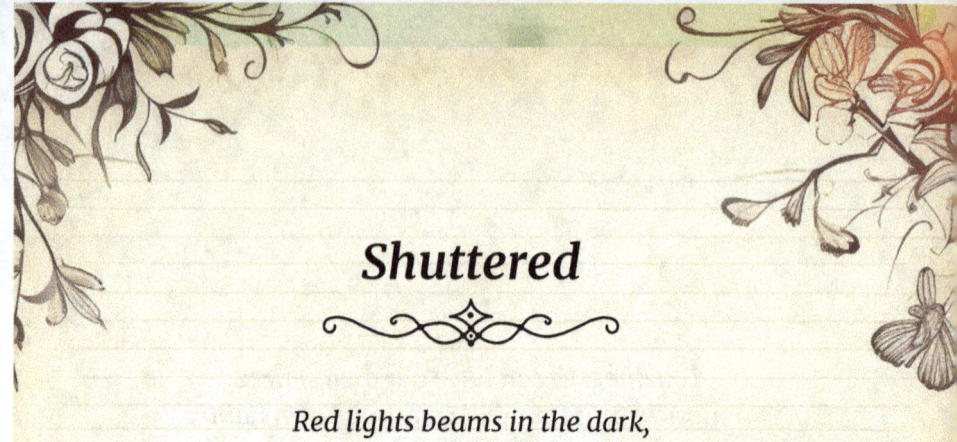

Shuttered

Red lights beams in the dark,
Glowing slowly without a spark
Breathing heavy with slighter noise,
Engine sound and whisper voice

Lights keeps beaming,
And my heart keeps beating.
Death upon arrival,
Manoeuvre with a live vein.

Stalkers by no means last a year,
They live to create fear.
Machine makes your trajectory clear
It ends slower than a delusion.

Breathe rate haste wilder in blood
Glowing red to make a bright vision
Darkness' is more life to light
Happiness is crueler than anger.

The did gross do what's done
The end is the painting on the wall.

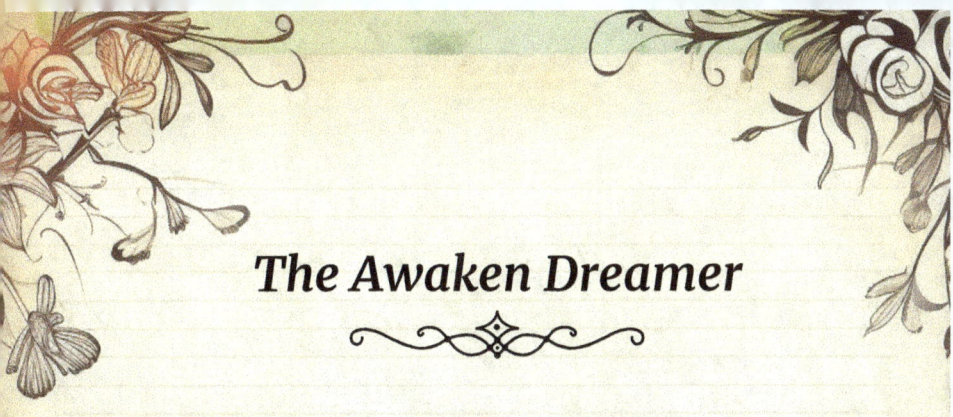

The Awaken Dreamer

It is a sanctuary to be gone
However, you're not left alone
Because we are all at our own
The different lies in our zones
Nevertheless, I promise to be a reborn

I subjected my life on others
Transmuting everything I live for to take
You are here and we cannot fight it
Driven by surprises on why can't we...
We can destroy it by bowing for him above

Our spirits can rise before our ancestors
To build our strength past Samson's muscle
We always scream and he listens
You can confide us but we keep on counting
It is not about us but it is sinners in us
They live to bind their own rules,

However, we all know who the real ruler is
Hiding in their temples of old cages
Like Sodom and Gomorrah's disappearance
Yes, you came in and yes, you can't win but lavish

Covid – 19

Superficially, you are not a magician
Thus far, you smell like a blabbermouth
Dazzled in our arena,
With a big scar like the walking dead

We are now your free sandwich
That is so sweet and luscious
Free from coquetting our belly
We got brown eyes and red lips with wide hips,

You got blue eyes and clown lips with a smile to sip.
Laugh out all loud until we will burst my ribs.
Flying a flywheel at risk
Yet, we know that we are getting sick

Crying for venting to cooldown ourselves
Yet we continue crawling to our safety
Because we know, corona is feisty.
At this point, we are all afraid...
Because you're never humble to be our friend

Hope as a Gift

Likes can be more likeable to those with like fortune-teller
Loosing a free will is a freedom to those with a pure heart
Just imagine, born poor and pursue a great life journey
It's his will to see and know your purpose
Thus, we have to remember our paths,
Our body remain tinted with a bright light.

It's a lamp that can remove us from darkness's
It's a free journey, a life journey of all time.
What we need now is a direction,
And what we have so far is just a hope
If we have to ask for anything then its faith that we need.
Our life is driven by our worse punisher of the underworld

We don't build trust to rust.
Now I see you and I'll please you.
You can hear me but you fear for me
Sadistic voices had hit my ears, just to keep your voice near.
And together we can live for many reasons
Our journey starts next season, everyday comes ever ready.

That's why I'm afraid to rise, because power is like a rose.
A day to plant it and a day it dry out

We both love this life, and in this life is to be alive.
Likes can be more likeable if you're reliable
My existent is my reality,
And my words are the extreme act of my blessing

I'm not a Fool

From the time you became my idea
You pretended to be here
I have learned to know your past
Even your past impostor years

I learned about your lies
Kept in a hidden file
Off-course it's all over your face
Trying to cage me in a quiet space

You gave me words to believe
I believed and felt relieve
Lying with a humble heart
It's all about me to get hurt

Giving the same excuses to last
While fooling with my past
But your secret is not fictions
Because you enjoy such actions

I am bad because I asked,
And left trembled with what you're tasked
But now you're sorry because I know
While my story is yet to be known

The Wrath of a Girlygirl

What am I if...?
I can't be myself to last
What if I'm the shadow?
A body without an image
My imagination can be a turning wheel
Rolling even things I can't remember

Who can I be if...
Maybe a space in between,
A diver between waves,
A sinner between two wives,
A beginner among thieves,
Or an Angel that save lives.

What can I be if...
I see a dragon without wings,
See a Queen without a King,
Or at least a champion in the ring
But remain cheap in her blanket.
It's a spiral voice on hard truth.

About the Author

Ladislaus Haindaka Munango, a native of Namibia's vibrant Kavango East region, is a storyteller whose pen breathes life into words. With a fervent belief in the transformative power of writing, he aspires to inspire and sculpt the lives of many. His dual role as an educator has refined his craft, allowing him to weave his personal experiences into narratives that resonate with authenticity and depth. Each piece is a reflection of his own odyssey and the universal struggles we all face, lending his work an undeniable potency. As you turn the pages of his creations, anticipate a journey that will linger long after the last word is read. Stay tuned for his forthcoming works, which promise to etch an indelible mark on the literary world.

www.ingramcontent.com/pod-product-compliance
Lightning Source LLC
Chambersburg PA
CBHW070440010526
44118CB00014B/2124